Walking Through the Wilderness

Poems from the Author of "Only Jesus"

Illustrated with Photographs from the Holy Land

*"Thou shalt guide me
with Thy counsel,
and afterward receive me
to glory."*
Psalm 73:24

Copyright © 2019 Emily Hayden
Permission granted to copy and distribute
individual poems for personal use.
ISBN: 978-0-9961932-2-1

All photographs © 2018 by Emily Hayden.
S.D.G.

All Scripture quotations taken from the King
James Version of the Bible.

Table of Contents

Author's Note	9
Walking Through the Wilderness	13
Forth as Gold	17
He Restoreth My Soul	18
Love's Plan	23
You are My Shepherd	27
Those Gone Before	28
One Thing	35
On Winds of Truth	39
Asking	40
Battles	43
Be of Good Cheer	46
He Goeth Before	49
Just for Him	53
Resilience	57
Strength as Your Day	59
The Mercy Seat	60
Hand in Hand	63
Song of the Upper Country	64
The Brook in the Way	67
Fulfillment	71

Of Nature's God	75
Partakers of His Holiness	81
Taken	85
A Birthday Prayer	91
Trust	94
Was Not This to Know Me?	97
Willingly Offered	101
Within Life's Busy Clatter	105
Lord Willing	107
Victory	108
Just Give it to Him	112
Wisdom's Prayer	116
Lost in Thee	123
The Ancient Land	125

Author's Note

This second book of poems is published with the same prayer as the first: that the words and lessons the Lord gave to bless and encourage me will encourage others in the same way to walk wholeheartedly with Jesus Christ.

I would like to give special thanks to the anonymous friends who gave my husband and me the spectacular wedding gift of a trip to the Holy Land. The photographs in this book are a tribute to their generosity.

*To my husband,
who first encouraged me to publish
these poems, and who shows me daily
what it is to walk with the Lord.*

Walking Through the Wilderness

*At the commandment of the Lord the children of
Israel journeyed...as long as the cloud abode upon
the tabernacle, they rested in their tents...but when
it was taken up, they journeyed.*
Numbers 9:18, 22

As walking through the wilderness
My Lord's own people went,
It must have looked to other eyes
A foolish, untaught enterprise,
To wait until a cloud should rise
Before they struck their tent.

A day, a week, a month, a year,
They tarried where they'd been,
While still the cloudy pillar stayed
And gave the tabernacle shade;
But on the day it rose, they made
Their journey once again.

The cloud led through the wilderness,
By ways both long and hard;
Although a quicker path lay near,
God sought to teach them trust and fear;

Before the battle's cry they'd hear,
They'd learn to know their Guard.

But though the way seemed pointless,
    long,
And strange to those around,
God gave them water from the rock,
With bread from heaven fed His flock;
And e'en as friend to friend would talk
With those His favor found.

So too my life may seem to some
A random, senseless trail;
But evidence tucked out of sight
Directs my path to left or right;
The One who leads me with His light
Is guiding without fail.

Forth as Gold

But He knoweth the way that I take: when He hath tried me, I shall come forth as gold.
Job 23:10

Oh, keep my eyes upon the prize
Your love has planned for me;
Don't let me stumble, slip, or trip
By looking round at what I see.

For things on earth that seem so real
Are fading fast away;
The unseen truths Your word reveals
Will hold eternal sway.

Though paths You've planned may crush
    my heart,
You don't afflict in vain;
Your own Son learned through suffering,
And glory gained through pain.

You know the way Your love has planned;
Your arms my steps enfold;
Through trials sharp, Your goal shines
    clear—
I shall come forth as gold.

He Restoreth My Soul

The Lord is my shepherd: I shall not want...
He restoreth my soul.
Psalm 23:1, 3

He restoreth my soul...
Oh, Redeemer on high,
Who yet dwells with the lowly
And guides with His eye,
My soul is worn out
With its own waffling ways,
And a surfeit of self
Dims bright hues into grays.

I am weary of weakness,
Of slips into sin,
Of finding what most I abhor
Deep within.
I hate what I love—
Selfish praise, worldly dreams—
I still crave what I know
Is but fool's gold's false gleams.

I am tainted, unholy,
Unwilling, unkind,

And the better I know me,
The worse "me" I find.
Oh, my Father, my Lord,
Pull my eyes off of me;
Turn my soul back to simple,
Full resting in Thee.

It should be no surprise
To find all dark within;
I am why Jesus died—
Hopeless, lost, born in sin.
But He makes my soul new;
Not just patched—fully whole;
For He gives me Himself;
"He restoreth my soul."

Love's Plan

My Lord, You know I love You so
Because You loved me long ago,
Before You laid the pillars of the world.
Before the Father and His Son
And Spirit, glorious Three in One,
Made man from dust, the plan of love
    unfurled.

You knew that man would choose to sin,
Reject Your love, and wallow in
His self-made slough of guilt and
    wretched pride.
But wanting love's free offering,
Not puppets dancing on a string,
You let him choose, and then—You came
    and died.

No other love can touch the feet
Of Him whose back the Romans beat—
Creator God, who held their very breath;
Who laid His power aside to die,
That we with Him might reign on high—
Impossible to grasp the height and depth!

Love's great redemption finished—done!
The plan of ages filled by One
Whose love for me I cannot comprehend.
A creature lost, defiled by choice,
He sought and called with love's pure
    voice,
And loved me to death's bitter, bloody end.

But as His death fulfilled the word
That ancient prophets wrote and heard,
So too that word decreed that He must rise.
The great I AM, eternal God,
The life, the truth, the light, the rod,
Destroyed His death and claimed the
    victor's prize.

The plan of love before my eyes
Unfolds, while glowing praises rise;
A panorama glorious, divine;
Eternal love, that, seeking me,
Would die for its worst enemy;
Oh, Savior, love above all love—take mine!

You are My Shepherd

You are my Shepherd, all I need;
You are my shield, my guide;
My soul's strong tower; in distress,
I climb to You and hide.

You are my Sovereign, heaven's King,
In gracious rule supreme;
I bow in utter worship, Lord;
Your love my heart's one theme.

You are my Savior; by Your blood
My spirit's ransom's paid;
The life You bought now live in me—
A full transaction made.

Oh, let me live for You, my King,
Your pleasure my command;
And keep me walking straight and true,
On toward Immanuel's land.

Those Gone Before

Those gone on before—
Oh, my Lord, what rich blessing,
To hear of Your faithfulness,
Your guiding hand.
You kept them till heaven,
'Midst angels confessing
That they were your people,
Your own chosen band.

Their footsteps I trace
As Your pierced feet they followed,
E'er finding You steadfast,
Sufficient, and kind.
You taught them and led them;
A cleft rock You hollowed,
For refuge in battle,
In heart and in mind.

They left You a record
Of promises honored,
Of miracles sent
When all earth's help was vain;
Of fellowship sweet,

When for Your sake they wandered,
Alone and forsaken,
In sorrow and pain.

Your love never failed them,
Your grace never faltered;
Impossible barriers
Melted like snow;
War's storm clouds You parted,
Men's stony hearts altered,
Sin's chains rent asunder
Your glory to show.

The shadowing wings
Of Almighty provision,
The comforting care
Of the Shepherd's strong rod,
Still follow those caught
By the heavenly vision,
Who firm in faith's vict'ry
Believe in their God.

My Harbor unchanging,
What fears can unmoor me?
Your power still reigns
O'er the world and the grave;

Let me follow the track
Of the faithful before me,
And join in Your conquest
The lost ones to save.

One Thing

The beauty of a single-focused life,
With just one goal, one hope, one love,
 one dream,
Sheds glory round the the sphere in which
 it breathes,
And kindles hunger with one passing
 gleam.
For just one thing on earth should claim
 our hearts,
Each aspiration clinging round that
 theme:
To know the One who gave Himself for
 us,
Who suffered all, His people to redeem.

No complicated task our Lord has set,
No convoluted track to twist our mind;
Just simple, undistracted, full pursuit
Of Jesus Christ, for all in Him we find.
A goal so plain, yet unattainable
For mortal men, however strong or fleet;
And yet a beauty so enchanting, sweet,
That captivated hearts all else resign.

A lifetime spent pursuing such a prize,
Though knowing it beyond all earthly
    grasp,
Counts all but loss if that ideal is gained,
And gladly chases on till life's last gasp.
One simple, glorious task—to know our
    King,
To join His suff'ring, holiness, and pow'r,
Till even death is swallowed up in joy,
And one with Him our Savior's hand we
    clasp.

On Winds of Truth

Oh, Lord, don't let my mind embark
On wandering worry's wavering ark,
To sail the deadly, dulling sea
Of "What will others think of me?"

No, Lord; their hearts I cannot know;
Conjecture's currents ebb and flow
On unwise waves of fancy's fear,
When by such shifting winds I steer.

Your word my compass, pointing true,
Yields bearings bound for pleasing You;
Your steadfast hand my rudder holds,
Your Spirit's light my chart unfolds.

Oh, let me sail life's daunting sea
On winds of truth, with eyes on Thee;
No fear of man to sway my soul;
Your love and holiness my goal.

Asking

"Ask, and it shall be given you; seek, and ye shall find; knock, and it shall be opened unto you."
Luke 11:9

I'm asking, Lord; oh, hear my prayer,
And grant my cry, my King;
And set Thy will in place of mine,
Though sharp the change may sting.

I'm seeking, Lord; oh, let me find
My heart's desire in Thee;
My quest to trust, obey, and rest—
A Christ-filled life my plea.

I'm knocking, Lord; oh, open wide
Your door of grace to me;
And send the answer to my prayers,
But first—send more of Thee!

Battles

Oh, set a guard before my mouth,
And guide my words, O Lord;
But more—bring back my errant thoughts
In line with Your pure word.

For as I think within my heart,
So is my true self shown;
No airy song, but battle drawn,
This world of thoughts I own.

A conflict stiff, unflagging, long,
With unseen dirk and pike;
There is no discharge from that war,
Till earthly tents we strike.

Cast down with ruthless, heartless hand
Imaginations vain;
And chop with double-sharpened sword
All lies that seek to reign.

But youthful lusts, desires strong,
Flee as from serpent's bite;

Nor stay to test their pow'r, but run
To Him who'll for you fight.

Oh, capture every thought, my Lord,
And test them for Your praise;
Let truth flow on unbroken, and
Let glory fill my days.

Be of Good Cheer

"Be of good cheer,"
Said my Lord to His friends,
When troubled and fearful they cried;
As He walked o'er the storm waves
That rolled as He ruled,
This word met their need:
"It is I."

"It is I;"
Perfect fullness, sufficiency, power,
Came toward them, subduing the sea;
And the love that called comfort
To men's storm-tossed hearts
Is the love that surrounds
Even me.

Oh, Savior, when I,
Frightened, lost, overwhelmed,
Feel the billows close over my soul,
Let me hear Your reminder
And be of good cheer;
You are here, ruling all,
Though waves roll.

He Goeth Before

And when he putteth forth his own sheep, he goeth before them, and the sheep follow him: for they know his voice.
John 10:4

As a shepherd e'er lovingly leadeth his flock,
He goeth before, He goeth before;
Across every valley, o'er every steep rock,
My Savior goes always before.

As a cloud in the daytime, a fire in the night,
He goeth before, He goeth before;
Walk on in His shadow, step sure in His light;
My Savior goes always before.

As the wind in the top of the mulberry trees,
He goeth before, He goeth before;
The battle is His; let Him fight, on your knees;
My Savior goes always before.

As you march to the war, sing His praise
    without fear;
He goeth before, He goeth before;
He can slay all your foes ere you ever
    come near;
My Savior goes always before.

In the throes of temptation, when heart
    seems to fail,
He goeth before, He goeth before;
He has blazed us a path; follow on
    through the veil;
My Savior goes always before.

Through the hallways of pain to the dark
    door of death,
He goeth before, He goeth before;
Glory streams through the portal! Oh,
    draw thy last breath!
My Savior goes always before.

Down the bright streets of heaven, alight
    with His sun,
He goeth before, He goeth before;
Eternity's wonders have only begun;
My Savior goes always before.

Just for Him

I do not wash the dishes,
Sweep the porch, or scrub the floor,
For a "thank you" from my family
Or a nice view from the door;
I do not straighten up the room
To have it neat and trim,
To impress the coming visitors—
I do it just for Him.

At least on my best days I do;
Sometimes my eyes will stray;
And then the tasks are empty,
And my joy will slip away;
Then work becomes a drudgery,
And plodding on grows grim,
Until my heart remembers
That I do it just for Him.

For then His strength will carry through
Whatever job He brings;
And even when the fish juice slimes the fridge
My heart still sings.

To do my work for love of Him
Is joy up to the brim;
And nothing is too hard to face
When life is just for Him.

Resilience

As flowers still bloom in springtime's
 fields of green,
Though whipped by sprightly breeze, and
 washed by rain,
Oh, may I bloom midst storm and flood
 serene,
Christ's sun within unclouded, earth's
 gales vain.

Strength as Your Day

Each day my Savior brings me,
He will give me strength to meet;
Each time I fail and stumble,
I but fall at His dear feet.

He lifts me up in kindness,
His love dries my foolish tears;
He pours His grace upon me,
Richer still with passing years.

Without Him I am helpless, lost,
And weak, and worn, and frail,
But in His quiet, daily power
Lies peace that can not fail.

For I am dead; a corpse of clay
No smallest move can make;
But Christ's indwelling life in me
All things can undertake.

Then let me leave myself behind,
Bleak, powerless, and dead,
And drink the daily, promised power
Of Christ, my Fountainhead.

The Mercy Seat

"And thou shalt make two cherubims of gold...toward the mercy seat shall the faces of the cherubims be."
Exodus 24:18, 20

As ever toward the mercy seat
The cherubs turned their face,
So hold my heart's unswerving gaze
On Your unchanging grace.

No grief too great, no sigh too small
To bring before Your throne;
In times of need, in days of joy,
I come to You alone.

The fast-closed holiest of all,
Christ's blood has opened wide;
With boldness born of Jesus' love,
I worship, plead, abide.

As cherubs bow in ceaseless praise,
So here on earth I kneel,
My soul at Your great mercy seat,
Your grace my spirit's seal.

Hand in Hand

Walking on a moonless night,
When stars are hanging low,
The last of twilight rimming hills
With gentle turquoise glow,
When all alone I stop to see
The beauty of my King,
The soft wind calls His love to me;
Tonight His song I sing.

As hand in hand I walk with Him,
His truth renews my heart;
Pain's grip slides free, deep sorrows flee;
Love salves each stinging dart.
As clean as all that wide, clear sky,
My soul stands in His grace;
As hope returns, my heart now yearns
For nothing but His face.

Song of the Upper Country

I sing of summer valleys,
And a pale blue summer sky,
Of redwing blackbirds' burbling song
On breezes drifting by.

I sing of cool, crisp autumn days,
Of hawthorn flaming red,
Of golden apples, plump fat quail;
Hay safely in the shed.

I sing of winter's frosty charm,
When farming work is done;
Of snowdrifts coaxed to sparkling gems
By icy winter sun.

I sing of springtime's bursting green,
Of daffodils and bees,
Of tiny, sprouting garden rows,
And trembling, brand new leaves.

I sing a song of valleys,
Full of beauty, toil, and love,
And send an Upper Country song
Of thanks to God above.

The Brook in the Way

"He shall drink of the brook in the way;
therefore shall he lift up the head."
Psalm 110:7

Along life's daily, winding way
Run waters pure and clear;
A crystal stream alive with grace,
And truth, and love, and cheer.

This flowing brook that follows me
Is He who loved me first;
A drink from His pure, flashing stream
Will quench the deepest thirst.

His waters hold the source of joy,
Of peace and boundless rest,
Of fortitude and stalwart strength
To stand life's sternest test.

His waters surge with power unknown,
Undreamed of, till I drink;
I tremble at the thunderous roar
While bowing at its brink.

And yet a still, small voice of love
Has called me to His shore;
The dusty, weary, earthly road
Has left me seeking more.

All things are offered in a draft
From living water's brim;
Unending love, pure hope, delight,
Forgiveness, heav'n, and Him.

To daily drink of Christ not only
Lifts life's crushing load;
The stream will then flow on through me
To others on life's road.

The One who gives all gifts to me
Will through me all things do;
It costs my all to drink of Him,
And count His promise true.

Along my way the waters flow,
More rich than mind can think;
My Savior calls me to Himself,
But—will I stoop and drink?

Fulfillment

Oh, Lord, how explain this new joy in my soul?
This sense of a deep, hidden longing made whole?
Of seeing the purpose for which I was made
Stepping out in the sun after years in the shade.

Of watching the heart that I placed in Your hand
Fully given by You to the man Your love planned;
This blending of lives long since given to You,
This merging of paths as they follow the True.

This oneness of hearts in full union with Thee,
As two yielded wills in Your truth are set free,

Free to love as You love, free to live as You lead,
Free to walk hand in hand, free in heart and in deed.

Free to follow in fellowship dearer than life,
Finding comfort in trouble and refuge in strife,
As each one in Your love makes the other complete,
And in joy unconstrained kneels as one at Your feet.

OF NATURE'S GOD

My Lord, I love you for your world—
Great craggy peaks, sunbeams unfurled,
And sweeping valleys banked by wood-
    lined hills.
I love you for the jet-black crow,
The new grass, green beneath the snow,
And for the nighttime cricket's cheerful
    trills.

I love you for the aspen trees
That tremble in the summer breeze,
And for the tiny, tumbling baby quail.
I love you for the buzzing bees
Bright pollen glowing on their knees,
And for the sunlight flashing on a sail.

I love you for the moonlight's gleam
That lights the sea a silvery stream;
I love you for the owl's haunting call.
I love you for the gulls that wheel
And dip, and soar, and cry, and squeal,
And for the red-gold maples in the fall.

I love you for the quiet fog,
The fallen, emerald-mossy log,
And for the deep, calm river's silent flow.
I love you for the ferns, laced gold
By evening sun in autumn's cold,
And for the velvet questioning-eyed doe.

I love you for night's friendly dark,
For rich, brown-russet, yellow-pine bark
Against the pine-bough green and deep
    blue sky.
I love you for the yellow rose,
The timid cottontail's twitching nose,
And for the great blue heron sailing high.

I love you for the crashing sea,
That mirrors your own constancy,
And for the red-rock canyons, ancient,
    strong.
I love you for the wind-blown wren,
Who cocks his bright black eye and then,
With farewell bow, leaves nothing but a
    song.

I love you for the sunny pool,
The weeping willows, gnarled, cool,
The meadowlark's sweet morning melody.
I love you for the shady brook,
The peaceful, still, sundappled nook...
I love you most of all, for—you love me.

Partakers of His Holiness

Partakers of His holiness—
O words that thrill my heart!
I know full well no work of mine
Can holiness impart,
But His—oh, Lord, to hide in You,
Your radiant white to wear,
Partaking of Your purity,
Your glorious grace to share!

I hunger, Lord, for holiness,
For pure, untrammeled love,
For justice, truth—the fruitful peace
Of wisdom from above.
No matter how I hunger, Lord,
And thirst for righteousness,
Your promise stands—I shall be filled;
Your word has pledged to bless.

Then let my soul, Lord, hunger on,
Its craving stronger still;
The more I long to be like You,
The more my life You'll fill.

Let all-consuming passion find
Fulfillment in Your grace,
My starving soul at last made whole
When first I glimpse Your face.

TAKEN

Oh, Lord, in my life things have come
    and have gone,
Some I loved, some I loathed, some I
    dreamed;
They were given and taken as Your love
    saw best,
However unsparing it seemed.

The pursuits as a child I followed with all
Of the reckless abandon of youth—
Oh, I loved them! And yet, as my heart
    turned to You,
They must die on the altar of truth.

As a girl I was caught by a lovely ideal,
That to reach cost great effort and pain;
But I gave it a place far too high in my
    heart,
And its loss was my undying gain.

I grew on, and the love of my musical soul
Was by injury snatched from my hand;

But the Giver of gifts gave me His choice
   instead,
And a blessing my thoughts never
   planned.

But one day all my love for those childish
   things
Came sweeping back over my soul;
And I fled to my room to escape to my
   Lord,
From the edge of a deep, grasping hole.

"Oh, my Father, You know I loved those
   most of all;
Did You have to take that very thing?"
Then His answer came back from a verse
   on my wall:
No gift without cost will I bring.

Oh, the joy that rushed in! What I'd given
   my Lord
Was the dearest my poor heart could find;
And the sacrifice made He had richly
   repaid,
As His light filled my life, soul, and mind.

For the off'ring of righteousness costs all
    I loved,
But that poor earthly dross I now spurn;
For the Lord in His love will take nothing
    away,
But He gives His own self in return.

A Birthday Prayer

For Ethel Jessup, 2017

My Lord, I ask You, for my friend,
A year of peace and grace;
A year of love's unclouded light—
The sunshine of Your face.

I ask for joy in You alone,
Unwavering and true;
For daily strength, the Spirit's power,
To run life's hard race through.

I ask for all fear lost in love,
All worry lost in trust;
All riches stored as jewels of gold
Above all earthly rust.

I pray for faith to look ahead,
For strength to finish well;
For calm dependence on Your word,
All inner storms to quell.

For eyes that, steadfast, look to You,
My Savior, glorious King;
That as my friend leads me to You,
You'll lead her heart to sing.

Trust

It isn't trust when all is clear,
When all is plain to see and hear;
But when the way grows clouded,
Then the time for trust draws near.

It isn't trust to worry, fret,
To say, "Yes, Lord," then add, "but yet..."
Or turn aside to doubting—
No! Trust's stand is firmly set.

It isn't trust to read God's word,
And then discount the message heard—
"All things for good," it tells us;
Joy ahead the cross endured.

It isn't trust that steals our joy;
But doubt will make us worry's toy;
Oh, fix your eyes up higher!
And the thrill of trust employ.

Was Not This to Know Me?

"Did not thy father eat and drink, and do judgment and justice, and then it was well with him?...Was not this to know Me?" saith the Lord.
Jeremiah 22:15,16

"Was not this to know Me?"
Asked the Lord of the king,
Pointing back to his father's right ways—
Doing judgment and justice,
Upholding the poor—
Virtues lost in the son's lustful days.

But the question was really
A statement of fact;
The king's deeds were a means to an end;
Idols crushed into dust,
Temple purged, laws renewed,
Were but seeking to know Abram's
    Friend.

There was no king before him
Who turned to the Lord
With such whole-hearted, whole-souled
    pure might;

Neither after would any
Arise in his place,
Till the King came who banishes night.

That king's life was beacon
Held out to his son,
Of the way that was well for his soul;
But the motive beneath
Holds the true goal of man:
To know Him by whose wounds we are
    whole.

Let me crush any idol
That rivals Your place
On the throne of all thrones in my heart;
Let me purge out the temple
Your Spirit indwells,
While Your great law of love rules each
    part.

"Was not this to know Me?"
Let my answer resound
From a life given over to You;
As I simply obey
Out of love every day
Let me know You in spirit and truth.

Willingly Offered

And they came...everyone whom his spirit made willing, and they brought the Lord's offering to the work of the tabernacle.
Exodus 35:21

Your people brought with perfect, willing heart
Brass, iron, silver, precious jewels, and gold;
Rejoicing as they offered, full and free;
So too my gifts are met with joy untold.

The precious jewels of moments, hours, and days,
I offer to my King, to take and use;
The gift of time He's given, I return—
No interruption shunned, no task refused.

The iron of my stubborn will I break,
And offer all its pieces up to You;
Oh, forge them into one unmatched desire
To seek Your will in all I say and do.

My empty, sounding brass to You I bring,
A vessel clanging, worthless on its own;
But scoured by grace, and tuned by living truth,
It rings abroad with love's clear, bell-like tone.

The silver cord of all my earthly life,
However long or short the spool may run,
I give to You, to draw it out at will,
Unwinding till my thread of time is done.

The gold of faith, Your freely given gift,
I offer e'en while fiery trial refines;
Oh, let me not resent the scorching flame,
But look beyond, where holiness is mine.

To offer willingly with perfect heart,
Is truly to rejoice in all I do;
For love casts out all doubt and slays all fear;
Pure peace have those that offer all to You.

WITHIN LIFE'S BUSY CLATTER

Within life's busy clatter, Lord,
Oh, let me hear Your quiet word,
And hold my heart still calm,
At one with You.

Let nothing shake the branch that bears
Your root's rich strength to slay my fears,
And let me watch in peace
Life's changing view.

While all around me chatters on,
Oh, set my inner gaze upon
The never-changing beauty
Of my King.

For though this world may clamor, cry,
Confuse, distract, divide, destroy,
Yet there within Yourself
I silent sing.

Lord Willing

Tomorrow I'm going to do something
    great,
Or quiet, or humdrum, or thrilling;
Something planned with an eye to my
    Savior's increase;
But never forgetting—
Lord willing.

For none of my plans are an end in
    themselves,
However worthwhile and fulfilling;
A man may mark out every step, every
    goal,
But the outcome depends on—
Lord willing.

In humble dependence on heaven's
    decrees,
Let my plans be Your Spirit's instilling;
Leaving room for Your wisdom to set
    them aside,
And with joyful trust adding—
Lord willing.

Victory

Oh, Lord, my King, tonight I've seen
You do what can't be done;
The heart I fought so hard to change
With Yours now beats as one.

These last two weeks I've battled, cried,
And fled behind locked doors,
To plead Your help and beg Your grace
While sobbing on the floor.

But now the battle's fled away
As dew before the sun;
My heart is resting in Your love,
Your quiet vict'ry's won.

With open face I raise my eyes,
With unencumbered soul;
With no desire on earth save You,
In freedom glorious, whole.

This battle wasn't won by me;
I'd fought and pled in vain;

Your mighty arm, by others' prayers,
My truant self has slain.

I have no words, my Lord, my King,
To praise You for such grace;
Release and freedom lift my heart,
Unburdened, to Your face.

'Twas just this lack of open gaze
That made these weeks a hell;
Now vict'ry's song soars skyward,
And as one with You I dwell.

Just Give it to Him

Why hold on so hard to your worries, my soul?
Why let long-ago insults and hurts take their toll?
No stewing or brewing can help or make whole;
No, my soul—just give it to Him.

Why look at the future with dread or despair?
Why feel so inadequate, dragged down by care?
Your strength is in Jesus—your burden He'll share;
Now, my soul—just give it to Him.

Why let fears overwhelm, why let brooding take hold?
Why stir up fresh fires from feuds long since cold?
Forgive, let it go—Christ gives mercy untold;
Hush, my soul—just give it to Him.

Why dredge up old failings, why dwell on past sins?
Why let doubting and guilt steal your joy deep within?
He has washed those away, a new life to begin;
Stop, my soul—just give it to Him.

Why not thrill to His call? Why not joy in His love?
Why not find all you seek as you seek Him above?
Life lived in His light outshines all you've dreamed of;
So, my soul—just give it to Him.

Wisdom's Prayer

A verse in James I read long years ago,
When seeking guidance, my life's road to know;
A promise made of surely answered prayer,
Of freely given wisdom, met me there.

But as I sought to follow that word's call,
To pray, and wait, and watch in wisdom's hall,
I learned in sterling truth the verse beyond—
To double-minded cries God won't respond.

For when my heart was purely set to do
Whatever task His wisdom pointed to,
I had His guidance, just as promised—sure,
Unwavering and calm, steadfast and pure.

But if deep down I wanted my own way,
And hoped I knew which choice His voice
    would say,
I met confusion's roil on every hand;
No answer came; no leading, no
    command.

Then, oh, the fight to kill that stubborn
    will,
And then with truly willing heart stand
    still;
The hours I spent at war with self, and
    lost;
The smallest choices hard-fought battles
    cost.

My will dies hard; I found I couldn't slay
My own desire—all I could do was pray,
"Lord, *make* me willing! Help me want
    Your way;
In Jesus' name, oh, cleanse my heart
    today."

And then at last, each time, He'd give the
    grace

To look with guileless heart into His face;
It cost me time and tears and much delay,
But oh, what joy to hear and then obey!

My will since then has not less stubborn grown;
I battle still before God's will is known;
But walking as He leads is worth it all,
And grace unending waits in wisdom's hall.

Lost in Thee

O let me lose myself in Thee!
No petty fear, no misery
Can touch the spirit hidden there;
No bondage, spite, resentment, care;
No longing unfulfilled I find,
When one with Thee in heart and mind.

For all I seek, or long to be,
Is found perfected, Lord, in Thee:
A selfless love, a quiet peace,
A strength that hardships but increase;
A steadfast truth, a wisdom deep,
A faith that climbs when paths are steep.

A joy untouched by time or place,
A mercy quick to offer grace;
An anger slow, ears swift to hear,
A heart that counts no gift too dear
To give the One who purchased me...
Oh, please, Lord, lose my self in Thee.

The Ancient Land

I've traveled in an ancient land,
Where empires rose and fell;
Whose cliffs and hills five thousand years
Of history could tell.

I've walked on stones that other feet
Millennia past have trod;
Yet their hearts beat, and felt, and lived,
As mine today, with God.

I've seen the blue-green, crystal waves
Of Joshua's Great Sea,
And stood where gladiators fought
And kings gave homily.

I've climbed an ancient, rock-strewn hill
And looked across the vale,
Where once a lad, strong in his God,
Goliath's boasts made fail.

I've scaled Megiddo's windy height,
Where ancient battles raged,

And scanned the plain where future man's
Defeat will end the age.

I've seen the sun-jewels flashing bright
On Galilean waves,
And heard the quiet breezes stir
Outside the shepherds' cave.

I've walked in teeming, jostling crowds,
And thought—they thronged Him, too;
I've seen a lonely mountaintop
And felt His solitude.

I've prayed in still Gethsemane,
"Thy will, not mine, be done,"
In consecration bowed anew
To Him whose vict'ry's won.

I've seen the skull of Calvary,
I've seen the empty tomb;
My heart has sung in speechless praise
The glories of my Groom.

And on the Mount of Olives,
Where my Savior wept and prayed,

I've thrilled to think He'll stand again,
In kingly robes arrayed.

I've gone up to Jerusalem,
I've passed where Jesus trod;
I've journeyed through the Promised Land,
And there I've walked with God.

-Jerusalem, October, 2018

www.ingramcontent.com/pod-product-compliance
Lightning Source LLC
Chambersburg PA
CBHW051601010526
44118CB00023B/2772